I Smell Chocolate

(Small Book)

~ Book 5 ~

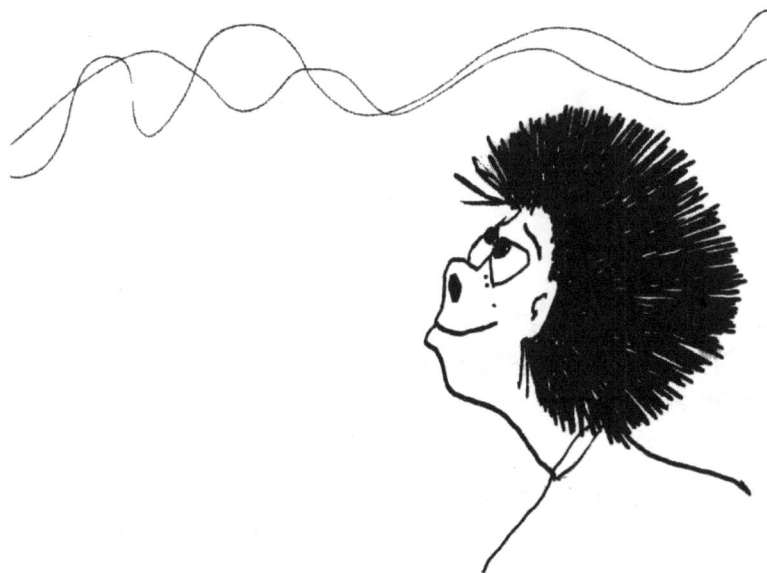

Peter Blueberry

Thank you for believing,

Olivia, Blake, Calvin,

Dane, and Rose.

I Smell Chocolate

Library of Congress Control Number: 2017951580

Table of Contents

Where Are My Socks

I can't find my socks anywhere.
I've got to hurry and put them on.
I'm late for my music lessons,
And Mom said not to take too long.

But, my socks aren't where I left them.
They're not outside on the lawn.
They're not under the bed or in my shoes.
And they're not where they belong.

But, I bet if I look really hard
I'll be able to find the proof.
I'll show my Mom that the ...
...sock monster's been here,
And put my socks ...
... upon the roof.

I think he eats...
... them too!

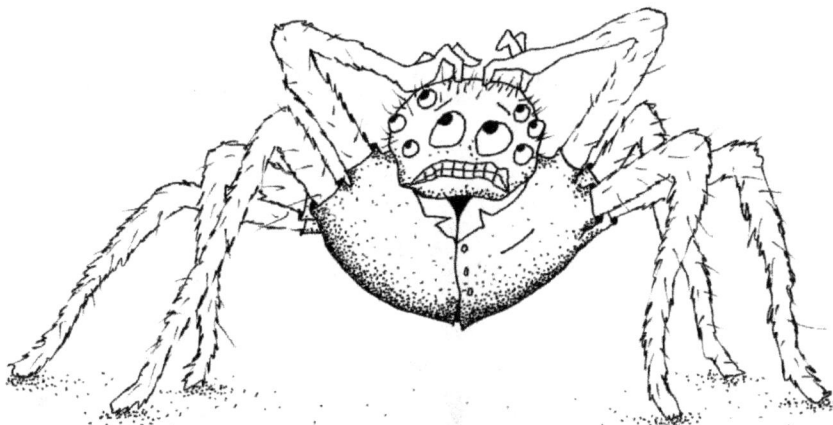

"Sider the Spider"

What's A Spider To Do

While I was walking to school one day,
I met a spider on its way.
To a meeting, it was going.
His distress it was showing.
He'd just gotten out of bed,
And this is what, to me, he said:
"If I get to the meeting way too soon,
I'll have to wait in a waiting room.
But, if I get there after one
I fear I'll be the only one.
But, if I sit where I can't see
I'll have to stand on someone's knee.
But, if they call on me to speak
I'm sure that it will make me freak.
But, if I turn around instead
I can go back home to bed.
Oh! I don't know what I should do.
Can I go to school **with you?**"

R   O   P   G   Y   B

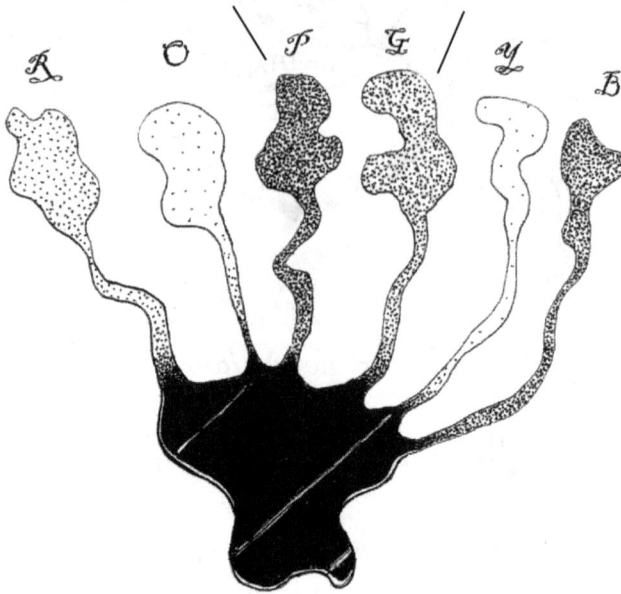

My Favorite Color

My favorite color is blue.
Or maybe it's really green.
But, I also like red a lot.
Now, that's a color that can be seen.

Or, what about the color purple,
Or possibly a nice light yellow?
I really do like yellow.
Yellow just seems so mellow.

Orange is also pretty.
Oh! I can't make up my mind.
What if I put them all together?
Oh! **Mud is what I find.**

Seeds

Daddy, there's a basketball
Growing in our garden.
Next to the roses.
Out where the yard ends.

It wasn't there yesterday,
So it grew overnight.
Can we grow some more?
Can we grow them tonight?

You can dig the holes,
And I'll rake the leaves.
Let's go get started.
All we need now are some . . .

. . . basketball seeds.

Who do you get basketball seeds from? A king!

The Giant And The Runt

Once there sat a happy giant,
And beside him sat a runt.
The giant laughed out loud.
While runt just gave a grunt.

The giant said, "Be happy,
And put your happy way up front."
The runt looked up . . .
. . . at the giant,
Then the runt . . .
. . . just gave a grunt.

Grunt . . . Grunt . . . Grunt!

A person needs to be happy,"
Said the giant to the runt.
"Being happy makes you grow.
Being grumpy makes you blunt."

"Laughing gives you energy,
And that helps you stand big and tall.
I've discovered that being happy
Is the best way to be of all."

"But there's one thing I should tell you."
To that the runt just gave a grunt.
"Did you know that once, I too,
Used to be a runt?"

The Bubble

I watched a bubble
Fall to the ground.
I crawled inside
To look around.

Then a wind blew up,
And I flew away.
Where I was going,
I could not say.

Over the trees,
And up through the air.
The view was splendid
Way up here.

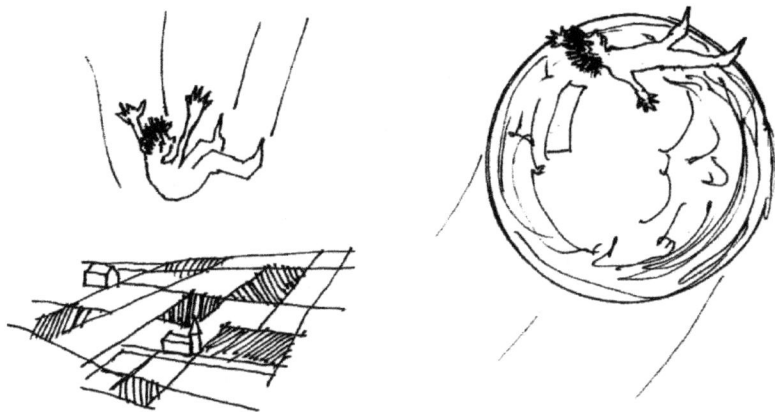

I saw things then
That I'd never seen.
Patchworks of land,
And colors so green.

All of a sudden
My bubble broke.
I fell through the air.
No longer to float.

Then I felt something
Squishy and soft.
Ah, it's another bubble
That's lifting me aloft.

Warm And Dry

It's raining on my window,
But so warm and dry inside.
The rain can't touch me now,
No matter how hard it tries.

I love to sit and watch
The water ribbons glide,
Slithering across the glass
Like snakes on a slide.

It just might rain all day,
Pouring from the sky,
So cold and dark and wet,
But so **warm and dry inside.**

Oops! That doesn't look like my tooth brush!

A New Day

I stubbed my toe on the bed,
And smashed my finger in the drawer.
I tore my shirt on the chair,
And spilled my milk on the floor.

My toothbrush fell in the toilet.
And I can't get my backpack open.
Can I please have a new day?
This one **seems to be broken.**

The Yawn

Why is my mouth wide open,
This gaping hole in my face?
I don't want people to see me,
I'm in a public place.

My mouth is doing something,
It does it over and over and again.
So I'd better get control it,
Or a bug's going to **fly right in.**

*I think I should have a
bit to eat before I
go to sleep.
Yawwwwwwwwwn!*

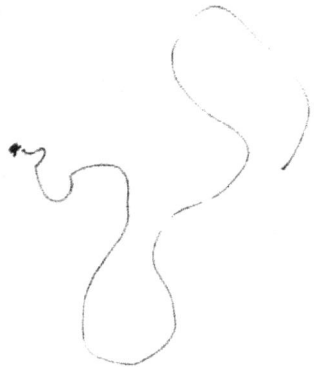

Are you ready to be my friend?

Are You Ready to Be My Friend

You don't have to build me up,
Or tell me how great I am.
You don't have to buy me anything.
Sometimes, just hold my hand.

You don't have to pat me on the back.
Just be someone I can depend.
Always tell me the truth.
Are you ready **to be my friend?**

Mmmmmm!

I Smell Chocolate

I smell chocolate.
I know there's some around.
Yup! I can smell chocolate,
It's just waiting to be found.
I know it can't be far,
And I'll search until I find,
That sweet and juicy morsel.
I can see it in my mind.
It will do no good to hide it,
That's what I'm going to say.
Cuz I can smell chocolate
From 200 feet away.
So, I'm going to find it soon,
If you'd like to make a bet.
You can't stop me now.
Cuz **I can smell chocolate.**

Holes In The Sky

My Dad and I were outside
Looking at the night,
Gazing at the stars,
Wondering at all the lights.

He said the night sky
Was like a big black sheet,
With tiny little holes,
Everywhere you could see.

When he said this to me,
I was really surprised,
Because I didn't know
There were **so many holes in the sky.**

So, dad! Who
puts all the holes
in the sky?

The Butterfly

Have you ever seen a butterfly
Come out of its cocoon?
I have a chrysalis here,
And it's going to open soon.

It's an amazing thing to see,
When the butterfly opens its wings.
It's a marvel of nature,
How magical it seems.

But, don't try to catch it.
It doesn't want to stay.
Just let it have its freedom,
And **let it fly away.**

Coming soon
to a branch
near you.

The I Doctor

I went to see the eye doctor
Yesterday at noon.
I had to have my eyes...
...checked out,
So I sat down in his room.

He showed me a chart...
...on the wall.
On it were a bunch of Es.
All pointing in different...
...directions.
It looked so confusing . . .
. . .to me.

The test was for me to point
In the direction each E went.
So I looked as hard as I could,
And indicated where...
...each E bent.

When the examination. . . .
. . . was over
He said I passed with ease.
So why do they call him...
...an I doctor
When all he shows you are...

... a bunch Es?

Oh, the last line? Sure, 'Made in China'.

21

It's Time To Go To Bed

The time has come for you
To get into your bed.
Pull up tight the covers up,
And lay down your weary head.

But I don't want to go.
I want to stay up instead.
I think I saw something hairy
Moving under my bed.

Meet "Harry the Dust Bunny Monster".

I Didn't Forget

Where are my mittens?
They're not where they should be.
I couldn't have misplaced them,
That's just not like me.

Weren't they on the door?
I used them in December.
I didn't forget where I put them,
I just don't remember.

*I see
something I
can't quite
describe!*

Waterfall

(A boy talks to the waterfall)

Oh, Waterfall,
Waterfall,
How majestic is your view,

How tall you are,
How far you fall.
Does anyone care for you?

. . . .

(The Waterfall answers)

Yes, my friend,
Oh, my friend.
There is someone close by.

Near they are,
And care they do.
I'm watched with **an eagle eye.**

Just a little more practice. But, you're getting better.

I Shot An Arrow

I shot an arrow
Into the air.
It missed my Dad,
But parted his hair.

I'd better go practice,
And practice a lot,
Until I become
A better shot.

A Small Price

If I help you with your homework.
What will you give me?
If I help you with your spelling.
Will you pay my fee?

If I explain your math to you.
Do you know what my fee will be?
The price for all this help I give.
It' just a smile, that's all I need.

Want to play a game?

The Fever

I've got a fever.
But that's O.K.
I get to miss school.
No homework today.

I'll be here all morning
Just lying in my bed.
My stomach feels fine
I've no ache in my head.

I've got a new game,
And I like it a lot:
It's called, "Ha, ha. I've got a fever,
Whether I have one or not."

The Boy With Grass Hair

Henry Blare had grass for hair,
After sitting in a grass green chair.

Then Henry's hair turned to ice too,
After sitting in a chair painted ice blue.

Then Henry's hair turned into Jello,
When he sat in a chair painted Jello yellow.

Then Henry saw a chair painted fire red.
**HENRY! DON'T SIT DOWN THERE!
STAND UP INSTEAD!**

I must be careful where I sit my seat!

Birthday notice, Feb. 2011 . . .
Gift, July 2011 . . .

Am I Late Or Not

I sent you a birthday present,
But you say it was 6 months ago.
I'm sorry that I missed it.
I guess I didn't know.

But, if you look at it this way;
My shopping's already done.
I'm not late for your last birthday,
I'm just **early for your next one.**

Don't bother me now!
This tree's starting to
bloom!

QUESTIONS

4. WHERE ARE MY SOCKS
   A. Where are the socks? *On the roof with the Sock Monster*
   B. What was he late for? *Music lessons*
5. WHAT'S A SPIDER TO DO
   A. Where was the boy going? *To school*
   B. What did the spider want to do in the end? *Go to school with the child*
   A. What would happen if they asked him to speak? *He'd freak*
6. MY FAVORITR COLOR
   A. What's a color that can be seen? *Red*
   B. When put together, what color did they all make? *Mud*
7. SEEDS
   A. What kind of seeds were they? *Basketball*
   B. When did the basketball grow? *Overnight*
8. THE GIANT AND THE RUNT
   A. What did the Runt do? *Grunt*
   B. What did the Giant used to be? *A runt*
10. THE BUBBLE
   A. What did he do to the bubble? *He crawled inside and looked around*
   B. Where did the bubble go? *Over the trees and up through the air*
   C. What happened to the bubble? *It broke and he fell…onto another bubble*
12. WARM AND DRY
   A. What was he doing? *Watching the rain on his window*
   B. How long might it rain? *All day*
   C. What was on the window? *Water ribbons that looked like slithering snakes*
14. A NEW DAY
   A. What did he stub his toe on? *The bed*
   B. What happened to his toothbrush? *He dropped it into the toilet*
   C. What does he want? *A new day*

15. THE YAWN
   A. Where is he standing? *In a public place*
   B. What is going to fly into his mouth? *A bug*
16. ARE YOU READY TO BE MY FRIEND
   A. What does he always want you to tell him? *The truth*
17. I SMELL CHOCOLATE
   A. How far away can he smell chocolate? *200 feet*
   B. Why can't you stop him now? *Because he can smell chocolate*
18. HOLES IN THE SKY
   A. What are they looking at? *The night sky*
   B. What is the sky like? *A big black sheet with tiny little holes*
20. THE BUTTERFLY
   A. What is the butterfly in? *A chrysalis*
   B. What should you do to the butterfly? *Let it fly away*
21. THE I DOCTOR
   A. What was on the chart on the wall? *A bunch of E's*
22. IT'S TIME TO GO TO BED
   A. What's under the bed? *Something hairy*
23. I DIDN'T FORGET
   A. What was he missing? *His mittens*
24. WATERFALL
   A. Who is watching the waterfall? *An Eagle*
26. I SHOT AN ARROW
   A. Where did he shoot the arrow? *Into the air*
   B. What did it do to his Dad's hair? *It parted it*
27. A SMALL PRICE
   A. What was the price? *A smile*
28. THE FEVER
   A. Where was he? *In bed*
   B. What didn't he have? *A fever*
29. THE BOY WITH GRASS HAIR
   A. What was the color of his hair at first? *Grass green*
   B. Why did they want Henry to stand up? *So his hair wouldn't catch fire*
30. AM I LATE OR NOT
   A. What was he late for? *A birthday*
   B. What was he early for? *The next birthday*